Hooked On Math®
• Master the Facts •

WORKBOOK 4
DIVISION

Games and activities written by Leslie McGuire and Jennifer Trainor
Illustrations by Mitchell Rose
With special thanks to Thomas A. Romberg, Ph.D.; Mary K. Requa; Kit C. Land; and Melissa G. Lee, Ed.M.

Gateway Learning Corporation

Off We Go!

Dear Parents,
Welcome to *Hooked on Math* • *Master the Facts*, **Division**. In this part of the program, everything your child has learned in the previous levels comes together as part of a new skill: division. Here are some ideas to help your child grasp the concept.

Children divide all the time. Long before they enter school, children know what it means to share toys and treats equally. They understand that sometimes they don't have the right number of objects to go around for everyone, and so there are leftovers. Long division is just a way of sharing equally and seeing the leftovers on paper.

Division can be thought of as "undoing multiplication." If you've been playing the multiplication game by noticing groups of objects, like 3 dogs × 4 legs, you can show your child how to play the game in reverse. For example, divide the total number of legs by the number of dogs. Or count out 12 sticks of gum, and then have your child put them into 4 piles, counting how many sticks are in each pile. It can also help children to realize that they can go back and forth, checking their division answers by multiplying, and vice versa.

Because division and multiplication are so closely related, your child should have mastered all of the facts and skills from the previous three levels before beginning. If you think your child has forgotten some of these facts, please review them. With a strong foundation, division can be much easier, and more fun too.

Ready? Let's begin!

The Neptune Math Brigade

Division
How it works!

X's and O's Division Game
Try this simple game to explain division to your child.

What you need
Plastic sheet, special pen

How to play
1. Cover this page with the plastic sheet. Using the special pen, share 6 X's equally among the three circles below.

2. Count the number of X's you have drawn in each circle. That's the **quotient**—the answer in division.

Congratulations! You have just created a division equation! Try writing the problem and its answer in the green boxes at the bottom of this page.

If you'd like to play again, wipe off the plastic sheet, and try dividing 9 X's equally among the three circles. Then try dividing 12 X's, 15 X's, and 18 X's.

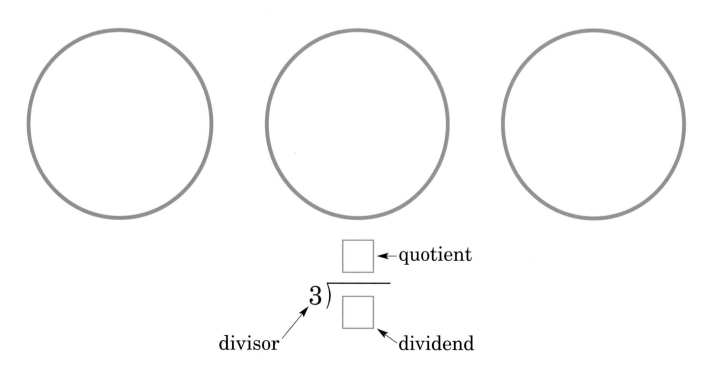

Division

How it works!

Division means to share equally. But it can also be the reverse of multiplication, or fast subtraction. If there are 15 fish, how many groups of 5 are there?

Try it:

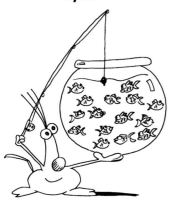    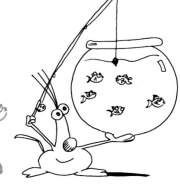

15 fish   minus 5 fish   are 10 fish,   minus 5 more fish   are 5 fish...

minus 5 more fish   is 0 fish.   There are 3 groups of 5 fish!

Division
How it works!

The **quotient** is the answer in a division problem.
The **divisor** is the number of equal groups you make.
The **dividend** is the number you divide equally.

Now, because you know all of your multiplication facts, you can check your division with multiplication. You will start by learning how to divide by 1. You will not learn to divide by 0 because it is not possible to divide by nothing.

Here's an example of how to check your answer:

Multiply the quotient $1\overline{)3}^{\,3}$

Check

by the divisor. $1\overline{)3}^{\,3}$

3
×1
3

The answer should be the dividend. $1\overline{)3}^{\,3}$

Dividing by 1

Listen to the green audio tape, side 1, lesson A.

Take out the green flash cards, side 1A.

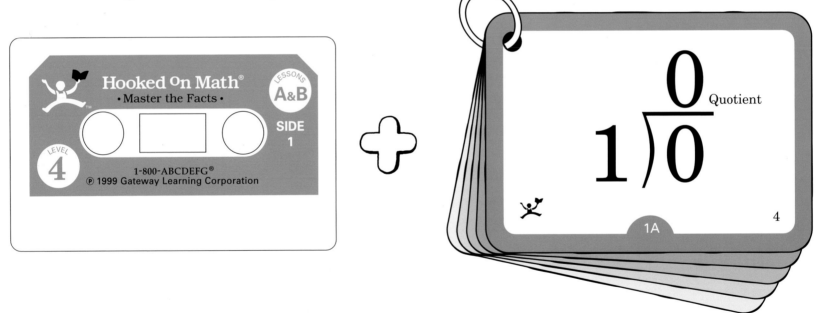

It's time to learn how to divide by 1. In this case, the quotient is always the same number as the dividend.

Practice and Check

Find each quotient and check.

Tip: The quotient is the answer in division. You can find the answers to all of the problems in this workbook in the *Parent's Guide*.

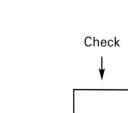

Check

Check

Check

$$1\overline{)0}$$
$$\times 1$$

$$1\overline{)1}$$
$$\times 1$$

$$1\overline{)2}$$
$$\times 1$$

$$1\overline{)3}$$
$$\times 1$$

$$1\overline{)4}$$
$$\times 1$$

$$1\overline{)5}$$
$$\times 1$$

$$1\overline{)6}$$
$$\times 1$$

$$1\overline{)7}$$
$$\times 1$$

$$1\overline{)8}$$
$$\times 1$$

$$1\overline{)9}$$
$$\times 1$$

$$1\overline{)10}$$
$$\times 1$$

$$1\overline{)11}$$
$$\times 1$$

$$1\overline{)12}$$
$$\times 1$$

When you get all of the answers right, put a sticker on ★1 on your poster.

Dividing by 2

Listen to the green audio tape,
side 1, lesson B.

Take out the green flash cards, side 1B.

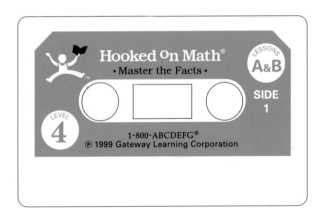

Hooked On Math®
• Master the Facts •

LESSONS
A&B

SIDE
1

LEVEL
4

1-800-ABCDEFG®
Ⓟ 1999 Gateway Learning Corporation

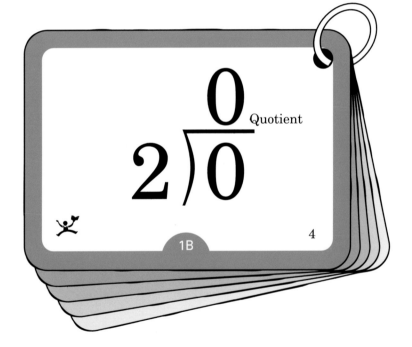

$$2\overline{)0}\,^{0}\text{Quotient}$$

1B   4

Dividing by 2 is the same as making one-half. For
all of these division facts the dividend is an even
number, but you can also divide odd numbers by
2. If you do, you'll always have one-half leftover.

Practice and Check

Tip: Dividing by 2 is the same as splitting in half.

Find each quotient and check.

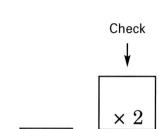

Check

$2\overline{)2}$ × 2

$2\overline{)4}$ × 2

$2\overline{)6}$ × 2

$2\overline{)20}$ × 2

$2\overline{)0}$ × 2

Check

$2\overline{)8}$ × 2

$2\overline{)22}$ × 2

$2\overline{)12}$ × 2

$2\overline{)10}$ × 2

Check

$2\overline{)14}$ × 2

$2\overline{)16}$ × 2

$2\overline{)18}$ × 2

$2\overline{)24}$ × 2

When you get all of the answers right, put a sticker on ★2 on your poster.

9

Review and Check

Dividing by 1 and 2

Find each quotient and check.

Check

Check

Check

Check

$2\overline{)22}$ $\times\,2$

$1\overline{)8}$ $\times\,1$

$1\overline{)3}$ $\times\,1$

$2\overline{)14}$ $\times\,2$

$2\overline{)4}$ $\times\,2$

$2\overline{)0}$ $\times\,2$

$2\overline{)18}$ $\times\,2$

$2\overline{)10}$ $\times\,2$

$1\overline{)6}$ $\times\,1$

$2\overline{)8}$ $\times\,2$

$2\overline{)20}$ $\times\,2$

$1\overline{)9}$ $\times\,1$

$2\overline{)16}$ $\times\,2$

$1\overline{)4}$ $\times\,1$

$2\overline{)6}$ $\times\,2$

$2\overline{)2}$ $\times\,2$

$2\overline{)12}$ $\times\,2$

When you get all of the answers right, put a sticker on ★3 on your poster.

Space Bingo™

Dividing by 1 and 2

How to play
For 1 or 2 players

1. The first player spins the spinner. The number it points to is the quotient.

2. The player matches the quotient with the correct problem on the game board. If the problem is already covered, the player spins again. Players alternate turns.

How to win
The goal is to cover three problems in a row, either horizontally, vertically, or diagonally. With 2 players, the first player to cover three in a row wins.

2)14	1)8	2)10
2)18	2)24	2)20
2)4	2)2	2)16
2)6	1)7	2)12
1)12	2)22	2)8

Dividing by 3

Listen to the green audio tape, side 2, lesson C.

Take out the green flash cards, side 1C.

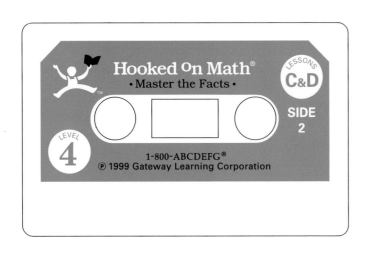

Division is multiplication in reverse. If each family at the beach has 3 children, and there are 27 children in all, how many families are there?

Practice and Check

Find each quotient and check.

Tip: Practice mental math! $3\overline{)36}$ is the same as $3\overline{)30+6}$. $3\overline{)30}$ is 10, and $3\overline{)6}$ is 2. $10 + 2 = 12$.

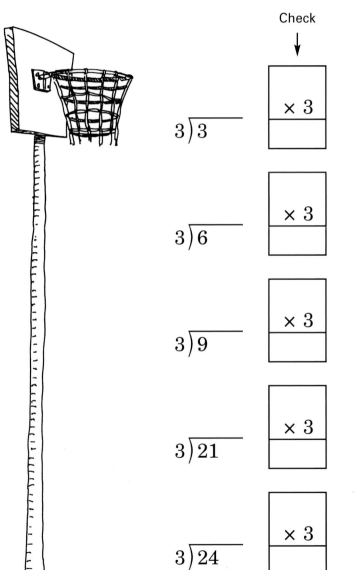

Check

$3\overline{)3}$ × 3

$3\overline{)6}$ × 3

$3\overline{)9}$ × 3

$3\overline{)21}$ × 3

$3\overline{)24}$ × 3

Check

$3\overline{)12}$ × 3

$3\overline{)15}$ × 3

$3\overline{)18}$ × 3

$3\overline{)33}$ × 3

Check

$3\overline{)30}$ × 3

$3\overline{)0}$ × 3

$3\overline{)27}$ × 3

$3\overline{)36}$ × 3

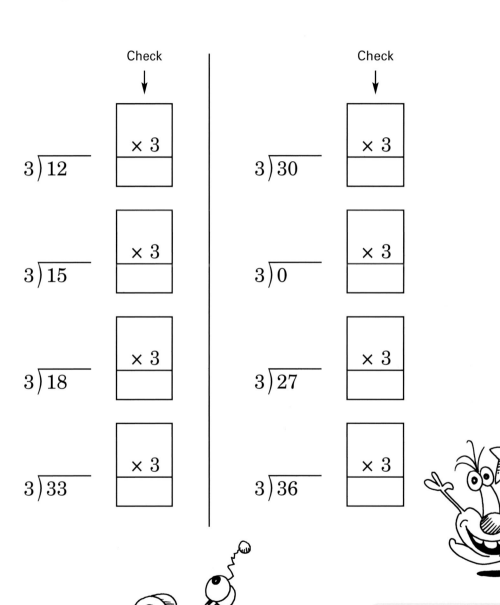

When you get all of the answers right, put a sticker on ★4 on your poster.

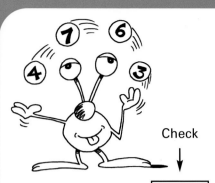

Review and Check

Dividing by 2 and 3

Find each quotient and check.

	Check		Check		Check		Check
$2\overline{)22}$	× 2	$2\overline{)18}$	× 2	$3\overline{)3}$	× 3	$3\overline{)30}$	× 3
$2\overline{)16}$	× 2	$3\overline{)6}$	× 3	$2\overline{)20}$	× 2	$2\overline{)14}$	× 2
$3\overline{)9}$	× 3	$3\overline{)18}$	× 3	$2\overline{)12}$	× 2	$3\overline{)12}$	× 3
$3\overline{)0}$	× 3	$2\overline{)10}$	× 2	$3\overline{)15}$	× 3	$2\overline{)8}$	× 2

Keep going! There's more!

Review and Check

Dividing by 2 and 3

Find each quotient and check.

	Check		Check		Check		Check
3)21	× 3	2)20	× 2	2)4	× 2	3)24	× 3
2)24	× 2	2)2	× 2	3)18	× 3	3)36	× 3
2)0	× 2	3)27	× 3	3)33	× 3	2)18	× 2
3)36	× 3	3)30	× 3	2)16	× 2	3)15	× 3

When you get all of the answers right, put a sticker on ★5 on your poster.

Space Bingo™

Dividing by 2 and 3

3⟌27	2⟌12	3⟌33	3⟌30
3⟌6	2⟌14	3⟌24	2⟌16
2⟌18	3⟌15	3⟌3	3⟌36
2⟌24	3⟌9	3⟌18	3⟌12

What you need
Game markers
Spinner

How to play
For 1 or 2 players

1. The first player spins the spinner. The number it points to is the quotient.

2. The player matches the quotient with the correct problem on the game board. If the problem is already covered, the player spins again. Players alternate turns.

How to win
The goal is to cover three problems in a row, either horizontally, vertically, or diagonally. With 2 players, the first player to cover three in a row wins.

Dividing by 4

Listen to the green audio tape, side 2, lesson D.

Take out the green flash cards, side 1D.

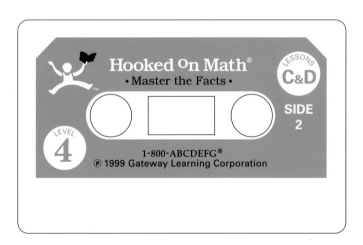

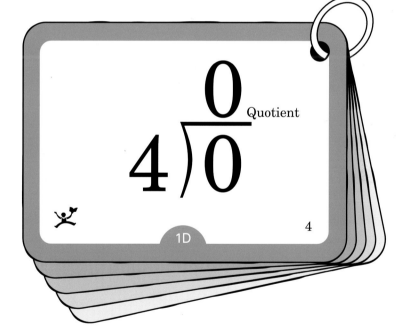

$$4\overline{)0}$$ Quotient

1D

4

Dividing by 4 is the same as making quarters. Think about things you divide into quarters—oranges, apples, dollars....

Practice and Check

Find each quotient and check.

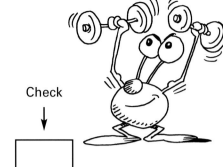

Check

4)4   × 4

4)28   × 4

4)20   × 4

4)48   × 4

4)32   × 4

Check

4)24   × 4

4)8   × 4

4)0   × 4

4)40   × 4

Check

4)16   × 4

4)36   × 4

4)12   × 4

4)44   × 4

When you get all of the answers right, put a sticker on ★6 on your poster.

18

Review and Check

Dividing by 2, 3, and 4

Find each quotient and check.

Tip: After your child has done the problems once, do them again and work for speed!

Column 1

Check ↓

4)40 | × 4 |

3)24 | × 3 |

4)12 | × 4 |

2)10 | × 2 |

2)8 | × 2 |

Column 2

Check ↓

3)27 | × 3 |

4)8 | × 4 |

3)0 | × 3 |

3)15 | × 3 |

Column 3

Check ↓

4)4 | × 4 |

2)6 | × 2 |

3)18 | × 3 |

4)20 | × 4 |

Column 4

Check ↓

4)48 | × 4 |

3)21 | × 3 |

4)16 | × 4 |

2)12 | × 2 |

Keep going! There's more!

19

Review and Check

Dividing by 2, 3, and 4
Find each quotient and check.

Check ↓

$4\overline{)28}$ × 4

$2\overline{)18}$ × 2

$3\overline{)27}$ × 3

$3\overline{)33}$ × 3

Check ↓

$2\overline{)16}$ × 2

$3\overline{)3}$ × 3

$4\overline{)24}$ × 4

$4\overline{)44}$ × 4

Check ↓

$3\overline{)15}$ × 3

$4\overline{)36}$ × 4

$3\overline{)30}$ × 3

$3\overline{)12}$ × 3

Check ↓

$4\overline{)32}$ × 4

$2\overline{)0}$ × 2

$3\overline{)9}$ × 3

$3\overline{)36}$ × 3

When you get all of the answers right, put a sticker on ★7 on your poster.

20

Space Bingo™

Dividing by 3 and 4

$3\overline{)36}$	$4\overline{)44}$	$3\overline{)27}$	$4\overline{)8}$	$3\overline{)30}$	$4\overline{)16}$
$4\overline{)48}$	$3\overline{)18}$	$4\overline{)36}$	$4\overline{)32}$	$3\overline{)12}$	$3\overline{)6}$
$4\overline{)20}$	$3\overline{)33}$	$4\overline{)4}$	$4\overline{)40}$	$4\overline{)12}$	$4\overline{)28}$

What you need
Game markers
Spinner

How to play
For 1 or 2 players

1. The first player spins the spinner. The number it points to is the quotient.

2. The player matches the quotient with the correct problem on the game board. If the problem is already covered, the player spins again. Players alternate turns.

How to win
The goal is to cover three problems in a row, either horizontally, vertically, or diagonally. With 2 players, the first player to cover three in a row wins.

Dividing by 5

Listen to the green audio tape, side 3, lesson E.

Take out the green flash cards, side 1E.

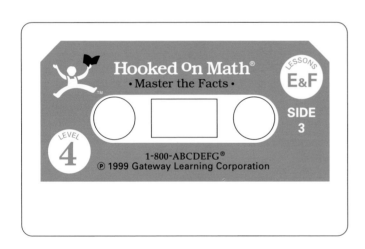

You can help your child learn how to divide by 5 by talking about things that come in 5s. If there are 25 fingers, how many hands are there?

Practice and Check

Find each quotient and check.

Check ↓

× 5	

$5\overline{)5}$

× 5	

$5\overline{)45}$

× 5	

$5\overline{)20}$

× 5	

$5\overline{)10}$

× 5	

$5\overline{)55}$

Check ↓

× 5	

$5\overline{)30}$

× 5	

$5\overline{)60}$

× 5	

$5\overline{)35}$

× 5	

$5\overline{)0}$

Check ↓

× 5	

$5\overline{)25}$

× 5	

$5\overline{)40}$

× 5	

$5\overline{)15}$

× 5	

$5\overline{)50}$

When you get all of the answers right, put a sticker on ★8 on your poster.

23

Review and Check

Dividing by 3, 4, and 5

Find each quotient and check.

Tip: If your child is having trouble, review the factors of 3, 4, and 5.

Check

$3\overline{)3}$ × 3

$4\overline{)32}$ × 4

$5\overline{)15}$ × 5

$5\overline{)50}$ × 5

Check

$4\overline{)36}$ × 4

$5\overline{)10}$ × 5

$3\overline{)12}$ × 3

$4\overline{)20}$ × 4

Check

$5\overline{)5}$ × 5

$5\overline{)60}$ × 5

$4\overline{)24}$ × 4

$5\overline{)0}$ × 5

Check

$4\overline{)48}$ × 4

$4\overline{)28}$ × 4

$5\overline{)20}$ × 5

$3\overline{)18}$ × 3

Keep going! There's more!

24

Review and Check

Dividing by 3, 4, and 5

Find each quotient and check.

Check

$5 \overline{)35}$ × 5

$3 \overline{)27}$ × 3

$4 \overline{)40}$ × 4

$5 \overline{)40}$ × 5

Check

$3 \overline{)24}$ × 3

$4 \overline{)4}$ × 4

$5 \overline{)45}$ × 5

$3 \overline{)21}$ × 3

Check

$4 \overline{)8}$ × 4

$5 \overline{)60}$ × 5

$5 \overline{)55}$ × 5

$4 \overline{)28}$ × 4

Check

$5 \overline{)25}$ × 5

$4 \overline{)44}$ × 4

$4 \overline{)32}$ × 4

$5 \overline{)50}$ × 5

When you get all of the answers right, put a sticker on ★9 on your poster.

25

Space Bingo™

Dividing by 4 and 5

5)60	5)20	4)48	4)8	5)5
5)45	5)25	5)55	5)40	4)44
4)36	5)50	4)4	5)30	5)10
4)24	4)20	4)32	4)16	4)20
5)15	4)28	5)35	4)40	4)36

What you need
Game markers
Spinner

How to play
For 1 or 2 players

1. The first player spins the spinner. The number it points to is the quotient.

2. The player matches the quotient with the correct problem on the game board. If the problem is already covered, the player spins again. Players alternate turns.

How to win
The goal is to cover four problems in a row, either horizontally, vertically, or diagonally. With 2 players, the first player to cover four in a row wins.

Dividing by 6

Listen to the green audio tape, side 3, lesson F.

Take out the green flash cards, side 1F.

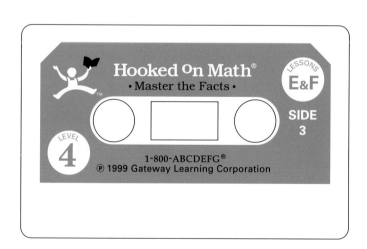

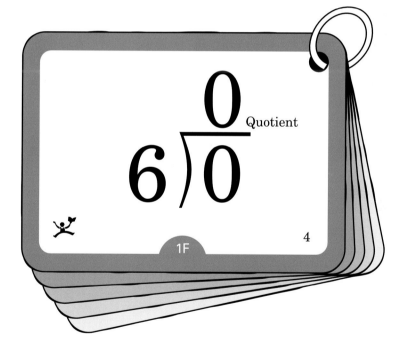

Remember the *Multiplication Station*™ song called "The Insect Dance"? What if you saw 24 insect legs? How many bugs would there be if each bug has 6 legs?

Practice and Check

Find each quotient and check.

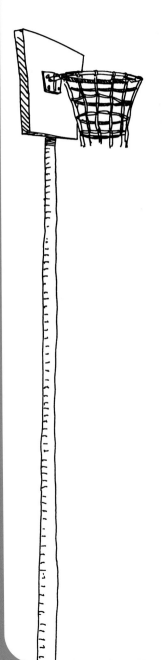

Check

$6\overline{)6}$ × 6

$6\overline{)48}$ × 6

$6\overline{)54}$ × 6

$6\overline{)66}$ × 6

$6\overline{)72}$ × 6

Check

$6\overline{)24}$ × 6

$6\overline{)18}$ × 6

$6\overline{)30}$ × 6

$6\overline{)0}$ × 6

Check

$6\overline{)36}$ × 6

$6\overline{)42}$ × 6

$6\overline{)12}$ × 6

$6\overline{)60}$ × 6

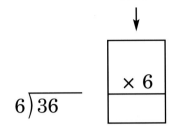

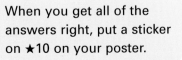

When you get all of the answers right, put a sticker on ★10 on your poster.

28

Review and Check

Dividing by 4, 5, and 6
Find each quotient and check.

Check

$4\overline{)4}$	$\times\ 4$

$6\overline{)60}$	$\times\ 6$

$6\overline{)6}$	$\times\ 6$

$4\overline{)8}$	$\times\ 4$

$5\overline{)40}$	$\times\ 5$

$6\overline{)12}$	$\times\ 6$

$4\overline{)12}$	$\times\ 4$

$5\overline{)35}$	$\times\ 5$

$6\overline{)18}$	$\times\ 6$

$4\overline{)16}$	$\times\ 4$

$5\overline{)30}$	$\times\ 5$

$6\overline{)24}$	$\times\ 6$

$4\overline{)20}$	$\times\ 4$

$5\overline{)55}$	$\times\ 5$

$6\overline{)30}$	$\times\ 6$

$4\overline{)24}$	$\times\ 4$

Keep going! There's more!

Review and Check

Dividing by 4, 5, and 6

Find each quotient and check.

Check   Check   Check   Check

6)42   × 6   4)32   × 4   5)20   × 5   6)0   × 6

4)36   × 4   5)25   × 5   6)54   × 6   5)35   × 5

5)45   × 5   4)48   × 4   6)72   × 6   5)40   × 5

6)48   × 6   4)28   × 4   5)60   × 5   6)66   × 6

When you get all of the answers right, put a sticker on ★11 on your poster.

Space Bingo™

Dividing by 5 and 6

5)‾20‾	6)‾36‾	5)‾10‾	5)‾55‾	6)‾30‾
5)‾5‾	6)‾54‾	6)‾72‾	6)‾42‾	5)‾40‾
6)‾36‾	6)‾6‾	5)‾50‾	6)‾12‾	6)‾48‾
6)‾24‾	5)‾15‾	6)‾18‾	6)‾66‾	5)‾30‾
5)‾35‾	5)‾20‾	5)‾40‾	5)‾25‾	6)‾60‾

What you need
Game markers
Spinner

How to play
For 1 or 2 players

1. The first player spins the spinner. The number it points to is the quotient.

2. The player matches the quotient with the correct problem on the game board. If the problem is already covered, the player spins again. Players alternate turns.

How to win
The goal is to cover four problems in a row, either horizontally, vertically, or diagonally. With 2 players, the first player to cover four in a row wins.

Dividing by 7

Listen to the green audio tape, side 4, lesson G.

Take out the green flash cards, side 1G.

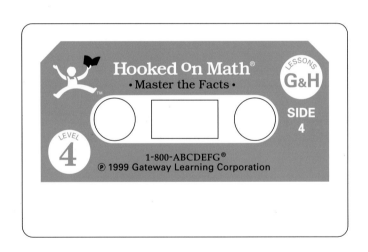

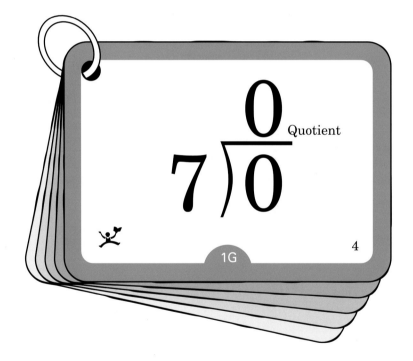

To help your child understand what it means to divide by 7, suggest counting the days until his or her birthday. Then ask your child to figure out how many weeks away it is.

Practice and Check

Find each quotient and check.

Tip: To reinforce understanding, use a separate sheet of paper and play the X's and O's Division Game on page 3 with 7 circles.

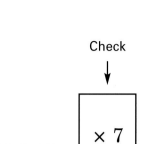

Check

$7\overline{)7}$ × 7

$7\overline{)77}$ × 7

$7\overline{)63}$ × 7

$7\overline{)14}$ × 7

$7\overline{)84}$ × 7

Check

$7\overline{)35}$ × 7

$7\overline{)21}$ × 7

$7\overline{)56}$ × 7

$7\overline{)0}$ × 7

Check

$7\overline{)28}$ × 7

$7\overline{)42}$ × 7

$7\overline{)49}$ × 7

$7\overline{)70}$ × 7

When you get all of the answers right, put a sticker on ★12 on your poster.

Review and Check

Dividing by 5, 6, and 7

Find each quotient and check.

Column 1

Check

6)24   × 6

6)48   × 6

7)21   × 7

7)77   × 7

Column 2

Check

6)54   × 6

7)14   × 7

7)70   × 7

6)72   × 6

Column 3

Check

7)7   × 7

5)60   × 5

6)36   × 6

7)35   × 7

Column 4

Check

5)10   × 5

6)42   × 6

7)28   × 7

5)30   × 5

Keep going! There's more!

Review and Check

Dividing by 5, 6, and 7
Find each quotient and check.

Check

$7\overline{)42}$ | × 7 |

$5\overline{)45}$ | × 5 |

$6\overline{)66}$ | × 6 |

$7\overline{)56}$ | × 7 |

Check

$5\overline{)40}$ | × 5 |

$5\overline{)15}$ | × 5 |

$7\overline{)84}$ | × 7 |

$5\overline{)20}$ | × 5 |

Check

$6\overline{)12}$ | × 6 |

$7\overline{)63}$ | × 7 |

$5\overline{)25}$ | × 5 |

$6\overline{)24}$ | × 6 |

Check

$7\overline{)0}$ | × 7 |

$5\overline{)30}$ | × 5 |

$6\overline{)30}$ | × 6 |

$7\overline{)49}$ | × 7 |

When you get all of the answers right, put a sticker on ★13 on your poster.

Space Bingo™
Dividing by 5, 6, and 7

What you need
Game markers
Spinner

How to play
For 1 or 2 players

1. The first player spins the spinner. The number it points to is the quotient.

2. The player matches the quotient with the correct problem on the game board. If the problem is already covered, the player spins again. Players alternate turns.

How to win
The goal is to cover four problems in a row, either horizontally, vertically, or diagonally. With 2 players, the first player to cover four in a row wins.

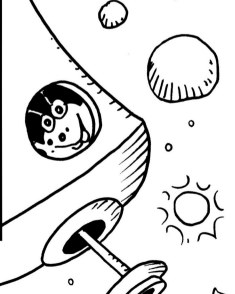

$6\overline{)42}$	$7\overline{)21}$	$7\overline{)35}$	$6\overline{)30}$	$7\overline{)63}$	$5\overline{)30}$
$6\overline{)54}$	$7\overline{)84}$	$6\overline{)72}$	$6\overline{)6}$	$6\overline{)24}$	$7\overline{)28}$
$7\overline{)42}$	$6\overline{)12}$	$5\overline{)40}$	$7\overline{)14}$	$6\overline{)18}$	$6\overline{)36}$
$6\overline{)60}$	$7\overline{)49}$	$6\overline{)66}$	$5\overline{)35}$	$7\overline{)56}$	$5\overline{)5}$

Dividing by 8

Listen to the green audio tape, side 4, lesson H.

Take out the green flash cards, side 1H.

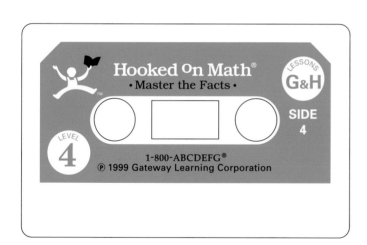

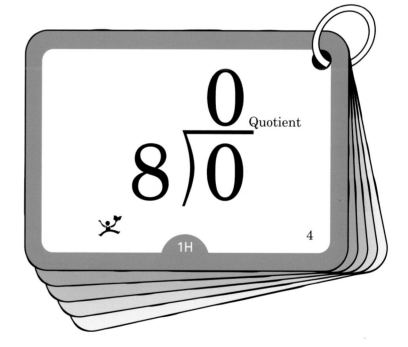

To help your child understand how to divide by 8, talk about sharing a pizza!

Practice and Check

Find each quotient and check.

Check ↓

$8\overline{)8}$ × 8

$8\overline{)96}$ × 8

$8\overline{)24}$ × 8

$8\overline{)16}$ × 8

$8\overline{)80}$ × 8

Check ↓

$8\overline{)32}$ × 8

$8\overline{)88}$ × 8

$8\overline{)48}$ × 8

$8\overline{)64}$ × 8

Check ↓

$8\overline{)56}$ × 8

$8\overline{)0}$ × 8

$8\overline{)72}$ × 8

$8\overline{)40}$ × 8

When you get all of the answers right, put a sticker on ★14 on your poster.

Review and Check

Dividing by 6, 7, and 8
Find each quotient and check.

Check

$6\overline{)6}$ × 6

$7\overline{)56}$ × 7

$8\overline{)24}$ × 8

$6\overline{)30}$ × 6

Check

$7\overline{)84}$ × 7

$8\overline{)16}$ × 8

$8\overline{)80}$ × 8

$7\overline{)35}$ × 7

Check

$8\overline{)8}$ × 8

$6\overline{)18}$ × 6

$7\overline{)42}$ × 7

$8\overline{)40}$ × 8

Check

$8\overline{)88}$ × 8

$7\overline{)49}$ × 7

$8\overline{)32}$ × 8

$6\overline{)36}$ × 6

Keep going! There's more!

Review and Check

Dividing by 6, 7, and 8
Find each quotient and check.

Check

$8\overline{)56}$ $\times 8$

$8\overline{)96}$ $\times 8$

$7\overline{)63}$ $\times 7$

$8\overline{)64}$ $\times 8$

Check

$6\overline{)48}$ $\times 6$

$7\overline{)21}$ $\times 7$

$8\overline{)48}$ $\times 8$

$6\overline{)42}$ $\times 6$

Check

$7\overline{)14}$ $\times 7$

$8\overline{)72}$ $\times 8$

$8\overline{)40}$ $\times 8$

$7\overline{)49}$ $\times 7$

Check

$6\overline{)36}$ $\times 6$

$6\overline{)54}$ $\times 6$

$8\overline{)0}$ $\times 8$

$6\overline{)72}$ $\times 6$

When you get all of the answers right, put a sticker on ★15 on your poster.

Space Bingo™

Dividing by 7 and 8

7)49	8)64	7)77	8)8
8)24	7)28	7)84	7)63
7)70	7)14	7)35	8)56
7)7	8)96	8)32	8)16
7)21	8)80	7)56	8)48
8)40	8)24	8)72	7)42

What you need
Game markers
Spinner

How to play
For 1 or 2 players

1. The first player spins the spinner. The number it points to is the quotient.

2. The player matches the quotient with the correct problem on the game board. If the problem is already covered, the player spins again. Players alternate turns.

How to win
The goal is to cover four problems in a row, either horizontally, vertically, or diagonally. With 2 players, the first player to cover four in a row wins.

Dividing by 9

Listen to the green audio tape, side 5, lesson I.

Take out the green flash cards, side 1I.

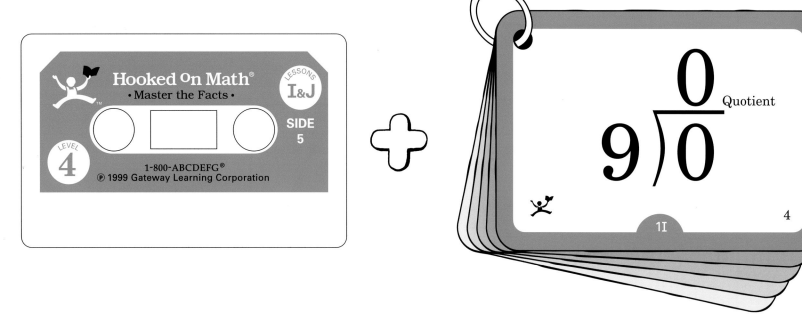

Think about when you need to divide by 9. How about when you are making up baseball teams?

Practice and Check

Tip: Practicing the factors of 9 can help make dividing by 9 easier. Listen to the *Multiplication Station* tape too!

Find each quotient and check.

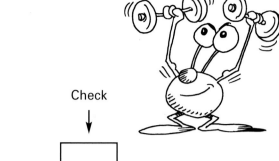

Check ↓

Check ↓

Check ↓

$9\overline{)9}$ × 9

$9\overline{)54}$ × 9

$9\overline{)0}$ × 9

$9\overline{)18}$ × 9

$9\overline{)108}$ × 9

$9\overline{)36}$ × 9

$9\overline{)81}$ × 9

$9\overline{)72}$ × 9

$9\overline{)63}$ × 9

$9\overline{)27}$ × 9

$9\overline{)90}$ × 9

$9\overline{)99}$ × 9

$9\overline{)45}$ × 9

When you get all of the answers right, put a sticker on ★16 on your poster.

43

Review and Check

Dividing by 7, 8, and 9

Find each quotient and check.

Check ↓	Check ↓	Check ↓	Check ↓

$7\overline{)84}$ ×7

$8\overline{)72}$ ×8

$9\overline{)9}$ ×9

$7\overline{)14}$ ×7

$8\overline{)64}$ ×8

$9\overline{)18}$ ×9

$9\overline{)99}$ ×9

$8\overline{)56}$ ×8

$9\overline{)27}$ ×9

$7\overline{)49}$ ×7

$8\overline{)48}$ ×8

$9\overline{)36}$ ×9

$9\overline{)90}$ ×9

$8\overline{)40}$ ×8

$9\overline{)45}$ ×9

$9\overline{)108}$ ×9

Keep going! There's more!

44

Review and Check

Dividing by 7, 8, and 9

Find each quotient and check.

Check ↓

$9\overline{)63}$ × 9

$7\overline{)56}$ × 7

$8\overline{)16}$ × 8

$7\overline{)84}$ × 7

$7\overline{)49}$ × 7

$8\overline{)32}$ × 8

$9\overline{)54}$ × 9

$7\overline{)42}$ × 7

$8\overline{)96}$ × 8

$9\overline{)81}$ × 9

$7\overline{)35}$ × 7

$8\overline{)40}$ × 8

$9\overline{)72}$ × 9

$7\overline{)28}$ × 7

$9\overline{)36}$ × 9

$9\overline{)108}$ × 9

Keep going! There's more!

Review and Check

Dividing by 8 and 9
Find each quotient and check.

Check

$9\overline{)72}$ $\times\ 9$

$8\overline{)48}$ $\times\ 8$

$9\overline{)36}$ $\times\ 9$

$8\overline{)24}$ $\times\ 8$

Check

$9\overline{)18}$ $\times\ 9$

$8\overline{)16}$ $\times\ 8$

$9\overline{)9}$ $\times\ 9$

$8\overline{)0}$ $\times\ 8$

Check

$9\overline{)54}$ $\times\ 9$

$8\overline{)96}$ $\times\ 8$

$9\overline{)45}$ $\times\ 9$

$8\overline{)64}$ $\times\ 8$

Check

$9\overline{)81}$ $\times\ 9$

$8\overline{)72}$ $\times\ 8$

$9\overline{)108}$ $\times\ 9$

$8\overline{)24}$ $\times\ 8$

When you get all of the answers right, put a sticker on ★17 on your poster.

Space Bingo™

Dividing by 8 and 9

9⟌63	9⟌36	8⟌24	9⟌9	8⟌96	8⟌64
8⟌32	8⟌8	9⟌108	8⟌56	9⟌81	8⟌88
9⟌18	8⟌48	8⟌72	8⟌16	8⟌80	9⟌72
9⟌99	9⟌90	9⟌54	9⟌27	9⟌45	8⟌40

What you need
Game markers
Spinner

How to play
For 1 or 2 players

1. The first player spins the spinner. The number it points to is the quotient.

2. The player matches the quotient with the correct problem on the game board. If the problem is already covered, the player spins again. Players alternate turns.

How to win
The goal is to cover four problems in a row, either horizontally, vertically, or diagonally. With 2 players, the first player to cover four in a row wins.

Dividing by 10

Listen to the green audio tape, side 5, lesson J.

Take out the green flash cards, side 1J.

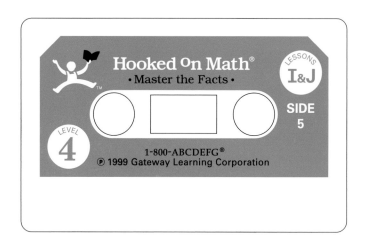

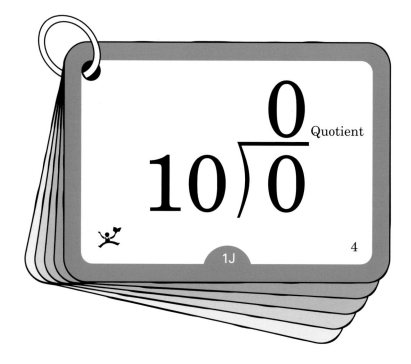

To think about dividing by 10, try making up a story using a dollar and 10 dimes.

Practice and Check

Find each quotient and check.

Check

Check

Check

$10\overline{)10}$ □ × 10

$10\overline{)0}$ □ × 10

$10\overline{)70}$ □ × 10

$10\overline{)110}$ □ × 10

$10\overline{)20}$ □ × 10

$10\overline{)50}$ □ × 10

$10\overline{)80}$ □ × 10

$10\overline{)120}$ □ × 10

$10\overline{)30}$ □ × 10

$10\overline{)60}$ □ × 10

$10\overline{)90}$ □ × 10

$10\overline{)100}$ □ × 10

$10\overline{)40}$ □ × 10

Review and Check

Dividing by 9 and 10

Find each quotient and check.

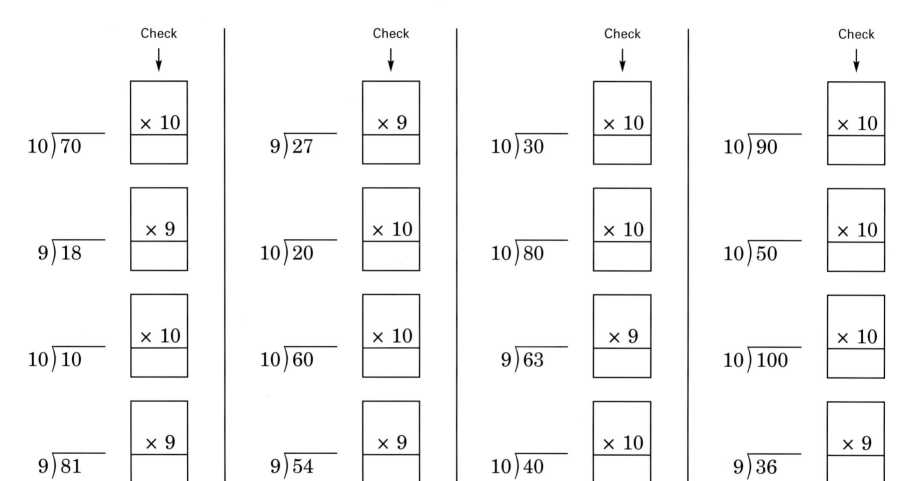

Check
$10\overline{)70}$ × 10

$9\overline{)18}$ × 9

$10\overline{)10}$ × 10

$9\overline{)81}$ × 9

Check
$9\overline{)27}$ × 9

$10\overline{)20}$ × 10

$10\overline{)60}$ × 10

$9\overline{)54}$ × 9

Check
$10\overline{)30}$ × 10

$10\overline{)80}$ × 10

$9\overline{)63}$ × 9

$10\overline{)40}$ × 10

Check
$10\overline{)90}$ × 10

$10\overline{)50}$ × 10

$10\overline{)100}$ × 10

$9\overline{)36}$ × 9

When you get all of the answers right, put a sticker on ★18 on your poster.

Space Bingo™

Dividing by 9 and 10

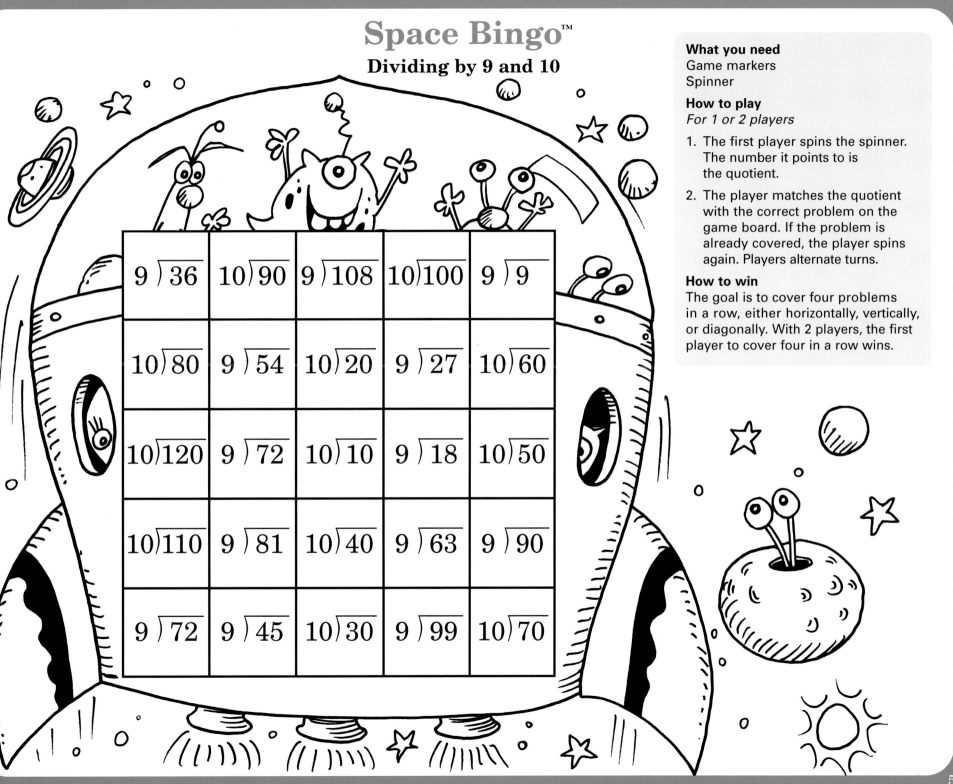

9)‾36	10)‾90	9)‾108	10)‾100	9)‾9
10)‾80	9)‾54	10)‾20	9)‾27	10)‾60
10)‾120	9)‾72	10)‾10	9)‾18	10)‾50
10)‾110	9)‾81	10)‾40	9)‾63	9)‾90
9)‾72	9)‾45	10)‾30	9)‾99	10)‾70

What you need
Game markers
Spinner

How to play
For 1 or 2 players

1. The first player spins the spinner. The number it points to is the quotient.

2. The player matches the quotient with the correct problem on the game board. If the problem is already covered, the player spins again. Players alternate turns.

How to win
The goal is to cover four problems in a row, either horizontally, vertically, or diagonally. With 2 players, the first player to cover four in a row wins.

Dividing by 11

Listen to the green audio tape, side 6, lesson K.

Take out the green flash cards, side 1K.

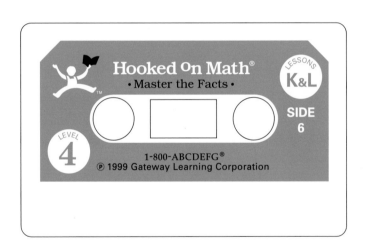

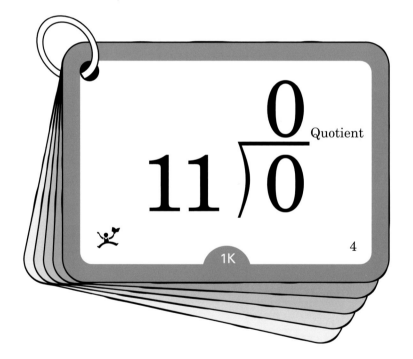

Often the basic division facts only involve divisors 1 through 10. We've included the 11 and 12 division facts to give your child extra practice.

Practice and Check

Find each quotient and check.

Tip: With the X's and O's Division Game on page 3, show your child why these problems seem easy. Draw 11 circles on a blank sheet of paper. Then share the dividend among the circles by drawing X's in each.

Check

11)11   × 11

11)55   × 11

11)22   × 11

11)99   × 11

11)66   × 11

Check

11)121   × 11

11)132   × 11

11)77   × 11

11)88   × 11

Check

11)0   × 11

11)110   × 11

11)33   × 11

11)44   × 11

Review and Check

Dividing by 10 and 11

Find each quotient and check.

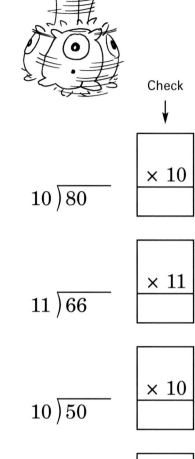

Check

$10\overline{)120}$ × 10

$11\overline{)22}$ × 11

$10\overline{)90}$ × 10

$11\overline{)55}$ × 11

$10\overline{)60}$ × 10

Check

$11\overline{)88}$ × 11

$11\overline{)11}$ × 11

$10\overline{)100}$ × 10

$11\overline{)44}$ × 11

$10\overline{)70}$ × 10

Check

$11\overline{)77}$ × 11

$10\overline{)40}$ × 10

$10\overline{)110}$ × 10

$11\overline{)33}$ × 11

Check

$10\overline{)80}$ × 10

$11\overline{)66}$ × 11

$10\overline{)50}$ × 10

$11\overline{)99}$ × 11

Keep going! There's more!

54

Review and Check

Dividing by 10 and 11
Find each quotient and check.

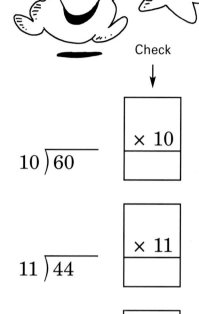

Check ↓

$10 \overline{)30}$ | × 10

$11 \overline{)121}$ | × 11

$11 \overline{)0}$ | × 11

$11 \overline{)55}$ | × 11

$10 \overline{)40}$ | × 10

Check ↓

$11 \overline{)11}$ | × 11

$11 \overline{)77}$ | × 11

$10 \overline{)10}$ | × 10

$11 \overline{)66}$ | × 11

$10 \overline{)50}$ | × 10

Check ↓

$11 \overline{)33}$ | × 11

$10 \overline{)110}$ | × 10

$10 \overline{)20}$ | × 10

$11 \overline{)132}$ | × 11

Check ↓

$10 \overline{)60}$ | × 10

$11 \overline{)44}$ | × 11

$10 \overline{)120}$ | × 10

$11 \overline{)110}$ | × 11

When you get all of the answers right, put a sticker on ★19 on your poster.

Dividing by 10 and 11

What you need
Game markers
Spinner

How to play
For 1 or 2 players

1. The first player spins the spinner. The number it points to is the quotient.

2. The player matches the quotient with the correct problem on the game board. If the problem is already covered, the player spins again. Players alternate turns.

How to win
The goal is to cover four problems in a row, either horizontally, vertically, or diagonally. With 2 players, the first player to cover four in a row wins.

$10\overline{)90}$	$11\overline{)55}$	$10\overline{)40}$	$11\overline{)22}$	$10\overline{)50}$	$10\overline{)80}$
$11\overline{)88}$	$11\overline{)121}$	$10\overline{)20}$	$11\overline{)99}$	$10\overline{)100}$	$11\overline{)33}$
$10\overline{)70}$	$10\overline{)10}$	$11\overline{)132}$	$10\overline{)60}$	$11\overline{)11}$	$11\overline{)77}$
$10\overline{)110}$	$11\overline{)44}$	$10\overline{)30}$	$11\overline{)66}$	$10\overline{)120}$	$10\overline{)70}$

Dividing by 12

Listen to the green audio tape, side 6, lesson L.

Take out the green flash cards, side 1L.

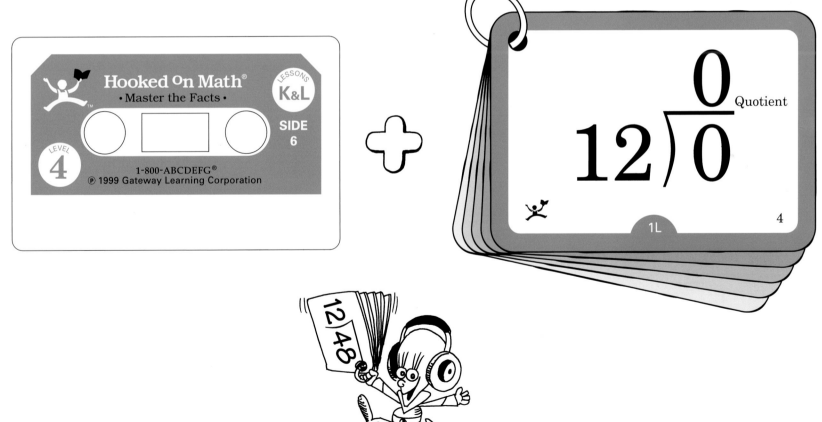

Practice and Check

Find each quotient and check.

Tip: Use an egg carton to demonstrate dividing by 12. It's important to reinforce sharing equally: Count out a factor of 12 beans, and distribute them equally in each section. The quotient is the number of beans in each section.

Check ↓

12)12   [ ] × 12

12)120   [ ] × 12

12)96   [ ] × 12

12)72   [ ] × 12

12)0   [ ] × 12

Check ↓

12)48   [ ] × 12

12)24   [ ] × 12

12)132   [ ] × 12

12)108   [ ] × 12

Check ↓

12)84   [ ] × 12

12)60   [ ] × 12

12)36   [ ] × 12

12)144   [ ] × 12

58

Review and Check

Dividing by 10, 11, and 12
Find each quotient and check.

Check ↓

12)0	Check ↓	× 12

$12\overline{)0}$ × 12

$11\overline{)132}$ × 11

$11\overline{)99}$ × 11

$10\overline{)20}$ × 10

$12\overline{)12}$ × 12

Check ↓

$10\overline{)50}$ × 10

$12\overline{)36}$ × 12

$11\overline{)121}$ × 11

$10\overline{)30}$ × 10

$12\overline{)24}$ × 12

Check ↓

$10\overline{)40}$ × 10

$11\overline{)88}$ × 11

$12\overline{)72}$ × 12

$12\overline{)48}$ × 12

Check ↓

$10\overline{)60}$ × 10

$11\overline{)77}$ × 11

$12\overline{)60}$ × 12

$11\overline{)110}$ × 11

Keep going! There's more!

59

Review and Check

Dividing by 10, 11, and 12

Find each quotient and check.

Check ↓

$11\overline{)44}$ × 11

$12\overline{)84}$ × 12

$10\overline{)80}$ × 10

$12\overline{)108}$ × 12

$10\overline{)120}$ × 10

Check ↓

$12\overline{)144}$ × 12

$11\overline{)11}$ × 11

$10\overline{)100}$ × 10

$11\overline{)66}$ × 11

$12\overline{)120}$ × 12

Check ↓

$10\overline{)70}$ × 10

$11\overline{)55}$ × 11

$12\overline{)96}$ × 12

$11\overline{)33}$ × 11

Check ↓

$10\overline{)110}$ × 10

$12\overline{)132}$ × 12

$10\overline{)90}$ × 10

$11\overline{)22}$ × 11

When you get all of the answers right, put a sticker on ★20 on your poster.

Space Bingo™
Dividing by 11 and 12

What you need
Game markers
Spinner

How to play
For 1 or 2 players

1. The first player spins the spinner. The number it points to is the quotient.

2. The player matches the quotient with the correct problem on the game board. If the problem is already covered, the player spins again. Players alternate turns.

How to win
The goal is to cover four problems in a row, either horizontally, vertically, or diagonally. With 2 players, the first player to cover four in a row wins.

$12\overline{)120}$	$11\overline{)44}$	$12\overline{)108}$	$11\overline{)99}$	$12\overline{)84}$
$11\overline{)88}$	$12\overline{)60}$	$11\overline{)55}$	$12\overline{)24}$	$11\overline{)132}$
$12\overline{)36}$	$11\overline{)121}$	$12\overline{)12}$	$11\overline{)22}$	$12\overline{)72}$
$11\overline{)33}$	$12\overline{)96}$	$11\overline{)110}$	$12\overline{)132}$	$11\overline{)77}$
$11\overline{)11}$	$12\overline{)48}$	$11\overline{)22}$	$12\overline{)144}$	$11\overline{)66}$

Let's Start Long Division!

Now that your child has mastered the division facts through 12, let's move on to more complex problems with larger numbers. Remember, division means to **share equally**, even when there are very large numbers involved. Be sure your child feels confident about the basic facts before beginning this section. It's important to build upon facts already mastered to be successful solving more difficult problems. Take each step slowly and practice, practice!

Long Division

How it works!

X's and O's Long Division Game

Try this version of a favorite game to explain long division to your child.

What you need
Plastic sheet, special pen

How to play
1. Cover this page with the plastic sheet. Using the special pen, share 39 X's equally among the three circles below. You can see that, as you draw the X's, you are subtracting from 39 over and over again.

2. Count the number of X's you have drawn in each circle. That's the quotient.

Congratulations! You have just created a long division equation. Try writing the problem and its answer in the green boxes at the bottom of this page.

If you'd like to play again, wipe off your plastic sheet, and try dividing 42 X's equally among the three circles. Then try dividing 45 X's, 48 X's, and 18 X's. You can also try making more circles on a separate sheet of paper and dividing these numbers again. (You might have some leftovers.)

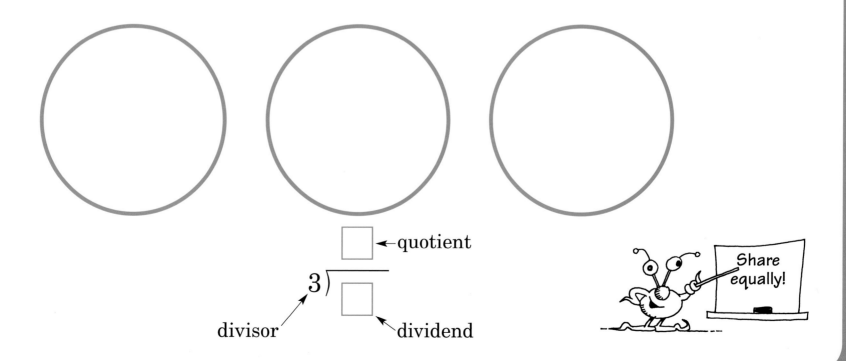

Long Division

With a 1-Digit Divisor and 2-Digit Dividend

Tip: Long division is really repeated subtraction. The steps below show a "shorthand" way to divide.

Here's how:

Step 1

Decide where to place the first digit in the quotient.

Are there enough tens to divide?

$$5 \overline{)55}$$

Step 2

Divide. Then multiply.

5 tens divided by 5 is 1 ten. Put a 1 in the tens place in the quotient.

$$5 \overline{)\underset{5}{55}}^{1}$$

Step 3

Subtract and compare.

5 minus 5 is 0. 0 is less than 5.

$$5 \overline{)55}^{1}\\ -5\\ \overline{0}$$

Step 4

Bring down the ones. Divide. Then multiply.

5 ones divided by 5 is 1. Put a 1 in the ones place in the quotient.

$$5 \overline{)55}^{11}\\ -5\downarrow\\ \overline{05}\\ 5$$

Step 5

Subtract and compare.

5 minus 5 is 0.

$$5 \overline{)55}^{11}\\ -5\\ \overline{05}\\ -5\\ \overline{0}$$

Step 6

Check your answer.

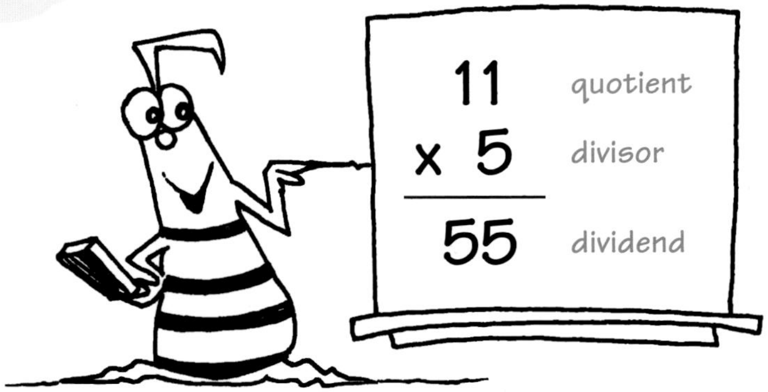

11	quotient
× 5	divisor
55	dividend

Practice and Check

Find each quotient and check.

Tip: Practice mental math! 5)‾5‾5‾ is the same as 5)‾5‾0‾ + 5. Divide each part of 55 separately, to get 10 + 1 = 11.

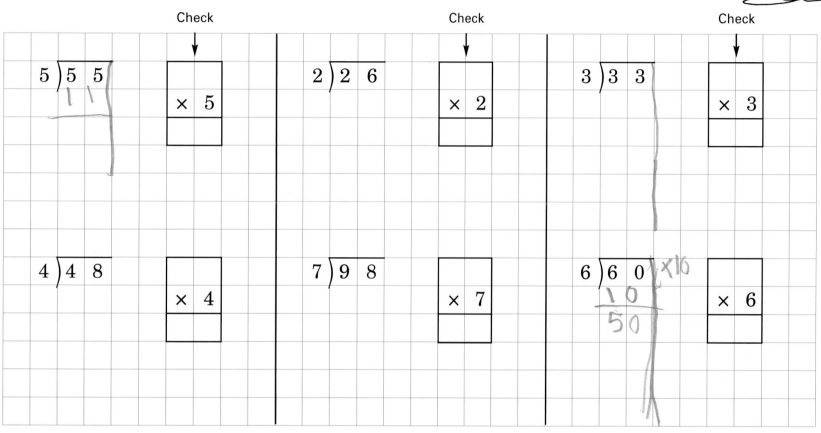

Check

$$5\overline{)5\ 5}$$

× 5

$$2\overline{)2\ 6}$$

Check

× 2

$$3\overline{)3\ 3}$$

Check

× 3

$$4\overline{)4\ 8}$$

× 4

$$7\overline{)9\ 8}$$

× 7

$$6\overline{)6\ 0}$$

× 6

65

Review and Check

Find each quotient and check.

Tip: Remind your child, "Remember to think about where to put the first digit in the quotient."

Check

$3\overline{)69}$ × 3

Check

$3\overline{)63}$ × 3

Check

$2\overline{)64}$ × 2

$3\overline{)93}$ × 3

$2\overline{)46}$ × 2

$4\overline{)48}$ × 4

$2\overline{)82}$ × 2

$3\overline{)39}$ × 3

$2\overline{)26}$ × 2

When you get all of the answers right, put a sticker on ★21 on your poster.

66

Leftovers

A Game of Remainders

Tip: Remainders are parts of a whole, like fractions of a pie. When you play this game, you may want to introduce your child to the concept of fractions. For example, if you have 6 pieces of pie, and 5 people each eat 1 piece of pie, you have 1 piece leftover—or $\frac{1}{6}$ of the pie.

Try this simple game to introduce remainders to your child. This game helps demonstrate how remainders work and shows that division is repeated subtraction.

What you need
15 game markers for each player
Spinner
Several sheets of paper
Pencil

How to play
For 1 or 2 players

1. The first player spins the spinner. The number the spinner points to is the number of circles the player should draw on the paper.

2. The player divides 15 markers into equal shares and puts the markers into the circles.

3. The player keeps any leftover markers—the remainders. This number is the player's score for this turn.

4. Players alternate turns 5 times, using a new piece of paper at each turn.

How to win
The player with the highest score after 5 rounds wins.

As your child becomes more proficient, increase the number of markers per player.

I had leftovers for breakfast,...

♫ ...leftovers for lunch,... ♫

...and ♫ leftovers for dinner, too-oo!

Long Division

With Remainders

Tip: The remainder in this example has another meaning: $\frac{5}{7}$. Take this opportunity to show your child how remainders are really fractions.

Here's how:

Step 1

Decide where to place the first digit in the quotient.

Are there enough tens to divide?

$$7 \overline{)89}$$

Step 2

Divide. Then multiply.

8 tens divided by 7? 1 ten is the closest answer. Put a 1 in the tens place in the quotient.

$$\begin{array}{r} 1 \\ 7\overline{)89} \\ 7 \end{array}$$

Step 3

Subtract and compare.

8 tens minus 7 tens is 1 ten.

$$\begin{array}{r} 1 \\ 7\overline{)89} \\ -7 \\ \hline 1 \end{array}$$

Step 4

Bring down the ones. Divide. Then multiply.

19 divided by 7? 2 is the closest answer. 2 times 7 is 14.

$$\begin{array}{r} 12 \\ 7\overline{)89} \\ -7\downarrow \\ \hline 19 \\ 14 \end{array}$$

Step 5

Subtract and compare.

19 minus 14 is 5. Put the remainder beside the quotient.

$$\begin{array}{r} 12 \text{ R5} \\ 7\overline{)89} \\ -7 \\ \hline 19 \\ -14 \\ \hline 5 \end{array}$$

Step 6

Check your answer.

$$\begin{array}{r} 12 \quad \text{quotient} \\ \times 7 \quad \text{divisor} \\ \hline 84 \\ + 5 \quad \text{remainder} \\ \hline 89 \quad \text{dividend} \end{array}$$

Practice and Check

Find each quotient and check.

$7\overline{)8\ 9}$ R

$\times$ 7

+   R

$2\overline{)2\ 3}$ R

$\times$ 2

+   R

$3\overline{)3\ 4}$ R

$\times$ 3

+   R

$4\overline{)4\ 6}$ R

$\times$ 4

+   R

$5\overline{)5\ 7}$ R

$\times$ 5

+   R

$6\overline{)6\ 8}$ R

$\times$ 6

+   R

Review and Check

Find each quotient and check.

Tip: Explain to your child that the remainder means part of a whole group—it is a fraction!

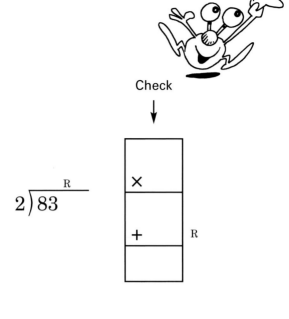

Check

$$3\overline{)64} \quad\text{R}$$

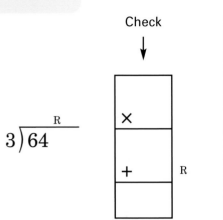

×	
+	R

Check

$$3\overline{)35} \quad\text{R}$$

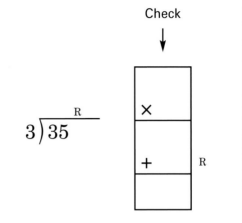

×	
+	R

Check

$$2\overline{)83} \quad\text{R}$$

×	
+	R

$$4\overline{)49} \quad\text{R}$$

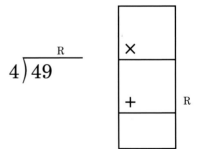

×	
+	R

$$2\overline{)47} \quad\text{R}$$

×	
+	R

$$3\overline{)94} \quad\text{R}$$

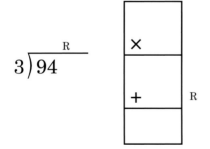

×	
+	R

When you get all of the answers right, put a sticker on ★22 on your poster.

Long Division

With a 3-Digit Dividend and a 1-Digit Divisor
How it works!

Tip: Children often have trouble understanding where to put the first number of the quotient. Try this simple activity to explain why the first number of the quotient may be placed in the tens column instead of the hundreds column.

What you need

1 dollar bill, 10 dimes, 10 pennies from the Money Bag

1 Ask your child to divide the dollar bill among 3 people. Explain that you can't divide the dollar, but you can divide 10 dimes, which equal 1 dollar.

2. Have your child exchange the dollar for 10 dimes, and ask your child to divide the dimes equally among three people.

3. Ask your child how to further divide the leftover dime. Suggest trading the dime for 10 pennies and dividing again.

4. Ask your child to show you how the answer in dimes and pennies matches the written answer to the problem.

How can you divide a dollar? With scissors?

Nope! Trade the dollar for dimes and pennies!!!

Tip: $7\overline{)334} = 7\overline{)300 + 30 + 4}$
$= 40 + 7\overline{)50 + 4}$
$= 40 + 7 + 7\overline{)5}$
$= 40 + 7 \text{ R5 or } 47\frac{5}{7}$

With a 3-Digit Dividend

$7\overline{)334}$

Here's how:

Step 1

Decide where to place the first digit in the quotient.

Are there enough hundreds to divide? No. Are there enough tens? Yes!

$7\overline{)3\,3\,4}$

Step 2

Divide. Then multiply.

33 tens divided by 7? 4 tens is the closest answer. Put the 4 in the tens place in the quotient. 4 tens times 7 are 28 tens.

$$\begin{array}{r} 4 \\ 7\overline{)3\,3\,4} \\ 2\,8 \end{array}$$

Step 3

Subtract and compare.

33 tens minus 28 tens are 5 tens.

$$\begin{array}{r} 4 \\ 7\overline{)3\,3\,4} \\ -2\,8 \\ \hline 5 \end{array}$$

Step 4

Bring down the ones. Divide. Then multiply.

54 divided by 7? 7 is the closest answer. Put the 7 in the ones place in the quotient.

$$\begin{array}{r} 4\,7 \\ 7\overline{)3\,3\,4} \\ -2\,8\downarrow \\ \hline 5\,4 \\ 4\,9 \end{array}$$

Step 5

Subtract and compare.

54 minus 49 is 5. Put the remainder beside the quotient.

$$\begin{array}{r} 4\,7 \;\text{R5} \\ 7\overline{)3\,3\,4} \\ -2\,8 \\ \hline 5\,4 \\ -4\,9 \\ \hline 5 \end{array}$$

Step 6

Check your answer.

$$\begin{array}{r} 4\,7 \quad \text{quotient} \\ \times\quad 7 \quad \text{divisor} \\ \hline 3\,2\,9 \\ +\quad 5 \quad \text{remainder} \\ \hline 3\,3\,4 \quad \text{dividend} \end{array}$$

Practice and Check

Tip: Watch for remainders!

Find each quotient and check.

Check

$$7 \overline{)3\ 3\ 4} \quad R$$

×

+ R

Check

$$6 \overline{)9\ 4\ 8} \quad R$$

×

+ R

Check

$$4 \overline{)4\ 9\ 2} \quad R$$

×

+ R

$$5 \overline{)8\ 9\ 2} \quad R$$

×

+ R

$$3 \overline{)3\ 3\ 1} \quad R$$

×

+ R

$$7 \overline{)9\ 8\ 9} \quad R$$

×

+ R

Review and Check

Find each quotient and check.

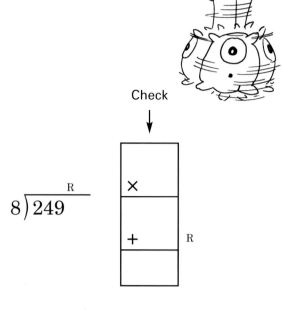

Check

$$9\overline{)739}^{R}$$

×	
+	R

Check

$$7\overline{)357}^{R}$$

×	
+	R

Check

$$8\overline{)249}^{R}$$

×	
+	R

$$9\overline{)469}^{R}$$

×	
+	R

$$3\overline{)217}^{R}$$

×	
+	R

$$4\overline{)324}^{R}$$

×	
+	R

Keep going! There's more!

Review and Check

Tip: Watch for remainders.

Find each quotient and check.

Check
$5\overline{)197}$ ᴿ

×	
+	R

Check
$4\overline{)349}$ ᴿ

×	
+	R

Check
$6\overline{)495}$ ᴿ

×	
+	R

$6\overline{)377}$ ᴿ

×	
+	R

$8\overline{)256}$ ᴿ

×	
+	R

$7\overline{)279}$ ᴿ

×	
+	R

When you get all of the answers right, put a sticker on ★23 on your poster.

Remainder Road

What you need
1 game marker for each player
Spinner

How to play
For 1 or 2 players (recommended for play with a parent)

Play begins on the first square.

The first player spins the spinner, divides the number on the game board by the number spun, and advances by the remainder. If there is no remainder, the player spins again. Players alternate turns.

How to win
The first player to reach the Finish square wins.

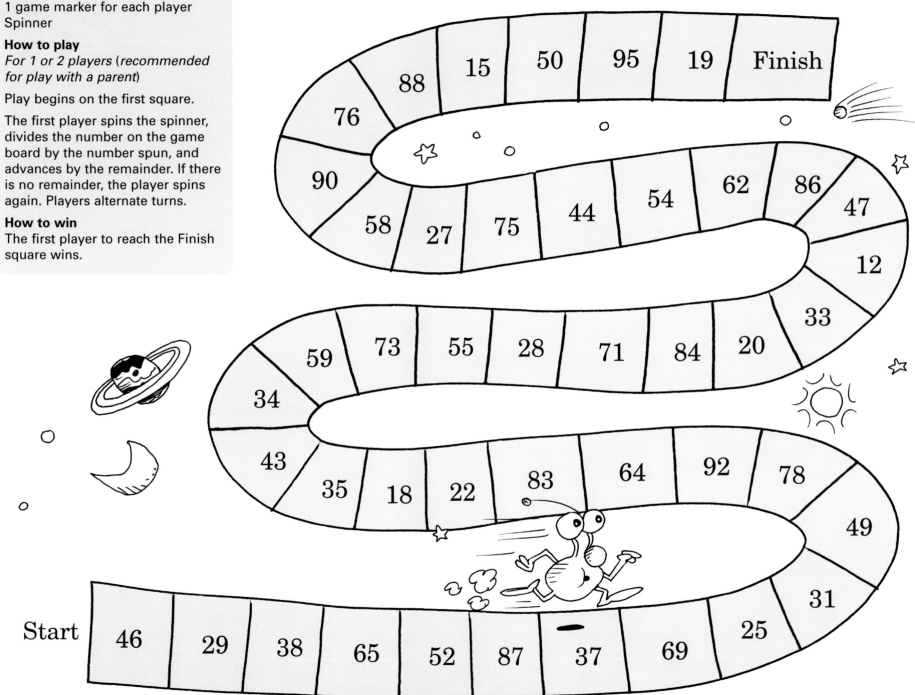

Start — 46 29 38 65 52 87 37 69 25 31 49

43 35 18 22 83 64 92 78

34 59 73 55 28 71 84 20 33 12

90 58 27 75 44 54 62 86 47

76 88 15 50 95 19 Finish

76

Long Division
With a Zero in the Quotient

Zero is a place-holder!

Here's how:

Step 1

Decide where to place the first digit in the quotient.

Are there enough hundreds to divide? Yes!

$$2\overline{)215}$$

Step 2

Divide. Then multiply.

2 hundreds divided by 2 is 100. Put a 1 in the hundreds place in the quotient.

$$\begin{array}{r} 1 \\ 2\overline{)215} \\ 2 \end{array}$$

Step 3

Subtract and compare.

2 minus 2 is 0.

$$\begin{array}{r} 1 \\ 2\overline{)215} \\ -2 \\ \hline 0 \end{array}$$

Step 4

Bring down the tens. Divide.

There are not enough tens to divide. Write zero in the quotient.

$$\begin{array}{r} 10 \\ 2\overline{)215} \\ -2\downarrow \\ \hline 01 \end{array}$$

Step 5

Bring down the ones. Divide. Then multiply. Subtract and compare.

15 divided by 2? The closest answer is 7. 7 times 2 is 14. 15 minus 14 is 1. Put the remainder beside the quotient.

$$\begin{array}{r} 107 \text{ R1} \\ 2\overline{)215} \\ -2\downarrow \\ \hline 015 \\ -14 \\ \hline 1 \end{array}$$

Step 6

Check your answer.

$$\begin{array}{r} 107 \quad \text{quotient} \\ \times\ 2 \quad \text{divisor} \\ \hline 214 \\ +\ 1 \quad \text{remainder} \\ \hline 215 \quad \text{dividend} \end{array}$$

Practice and Check

Find each quotient and check.

Check   Check   Check

R

2⟌2 1 5

×

+   R

R

3⟌3 2 7

×

+   R

R

5⟌5 2 8

×

+   R

R

4⟌4 2 9

×

+   R

R

5⟌5 5 1

×

+   R

R

6⟌6 5 1

×

+   R

Review and Check

Find each quotient and check.

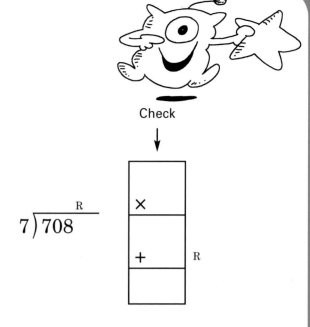

Check

$$4\overline{)400}^{\text{ R}}$$

×	
+	R

Check

$$8\overline{)810}^{\text{ R}}$$

×	
+	R

Check

$$7\overline{)708}^{\text{ R}}$$

×	
+	R

$$6\overline{)670}^{\text{ R}}$$

×	
+	R

$$7\overline{)780}^{\text{ R}}$$

×	
+	R

$$8\overline{)880}^{\text{ R}}$$

×	
+	R

When you get all of the answers right, put a sticker on ★24 on your poster.

Long Division

With a 1-Digit Divisor and a 4-Digit Dividend

$$6\overline{)4{,}339}$$

Here's how:

Step 1

Decide where to place the first digit in the quotient.

$$6\overline{)4{,}339}$$

Are there enough thousands to divide? How about hundreds?

Step 2

Divide. Then multiply.

$$\begin{array}{r} 7 \\ 6\overline{)4{,}339} \\ 42 \end{array}$$

43 hundreds divided by 6? What is the closest answer?

Step 3

Subtract and compare.

$$\begin{array}{r} 7 \\ 6\overline{)4{,}339} \\ -42 \\ \hline 1 \end{array}$$

1 is less than 6, so 7 tens is correct.

Step 4

Bring down the tens. Divide. Then multiply.

$$\begin{array}{r} 72 \\ 6\overline{)4{,}339} \\ -42 \\ \hline 13 \\ 12 \end{array}$$

13 tens divided by 6? What is the closest answer?

Step 5

Subtract and compare.

$$\begin{array}{r} 72 \\ 6\overline{)4{,}339} \\ -42 \\ \hline 13 \\ -12 \\ \hline 1 \end{array}$$

1 is less than 6 so 2 tens is correct.

Step 6

Bring down the ones. Divide. Then multiply.

$$\begin{array}{r} 723 \\ 6\overline{)4{,}339} \\ -42 \\ \hline 13 \\ -12 \\ \hline 19 \\ 18 \end{array}$$

19 divided by 6? What is the closest answer?

Step 7

Subtract and compare.

$$\begin{array}{r} 723 \text{ R1} \\ 6\overline{)4{,}339} \\ -42 \\ \hline 13 \\ -12 \\ \hline 19 \\ -18 \\ \hline 1 \end{array}$$

1 is less than 6, so 3 ones is correct. Put the remainder beside the quotient.

Step 8

Check your answer.

$$\begin{array}{r} 723 \quad \text{quotient} \\ \times \quad 6 \quad \text{divisor} \\ \hline 4338 \\ + \quad 1 \quad \text{remainder} \\ \hline 4{,}339 \quad \text{dividend} \end{array}$$

Practice and Check

Tip: Watch for remainders.

Find each quotient and check.

Check

6)4,3 3 9	R

×
+   R

Check

3)2,8 6 8	R

×
+   R

Check

5)3,6 9 2	R

×
+   R

2)5,1 4 2	R

×
+   R

7)6,7 8 8	R

×
+   R

9)4,0 5 9	R

×
+   R

Keep going! There's more!

Review and Check

Find each quotient and check.

Check
↓

$6\overline{)4{,}337}$ R ____

×	
+	R

Check
↓

$4\overline{)2{,}498}$ R ____

×	
+	R

Check
↓

$5\overline{)4{,}416}$ R ____

×	
+	R

$6\overline{)5{,}535}$ R ____

×	
+	R

$5\overline{)2{,}555}$ R ____

×	
+	R

$7\overline{)2{,}295}$ R ____

×	
+	R

When you get all of the answers right, put a sticker on ★25 on your poster.

Super Quiz
Math Magic

Try dividing the number 1,274,953,680 by any number up to 16.
(By the way, this number is made up of all of the numerals.)

You may want to use a calculator for this problem!

What happened? What is really unusual about this number?

How many numbers are really in this number?

That's a lot of dividing!

You can start with the easy numbers first!

Or start with the hard ones!

Wow!

See page 96 for the answer.

Long Division
With a 2-Digit Divisor and a 4-Digit Dividend

$12\overline{)2,654}$

Here's how:

Step 1
Decide where to place the first digit in the quotient.

$$12\overline{)2,654}$$

Step 2
Divide. Then multiply.

$$\begin{array}{r} 2 \\ 12\overline{)2,654} \\ 24 \end{array}$$

Step 3
Subtract and compare.

$$\begin{array}{r} 2 \\ 12\overline{)2,654} \\ -24 \\ \hline 2 \end{array}$$

Step 4
Bring down the tens. Divide. Then multiply.

$$\begin{array}{r} 22 \\ 12\overline{)2,654} \\ -24\downarrow \\ \hline 25 \\ 24 \end{array}$$

Step 5
Subtract and compare.

$$\begin{array}{r} 22 \\ 12\overline{)2,654} \\ -24 \\ \hline 25 \\ -24 \\ \hline 1 \end{array}$$

Step 6
Bring down the ones. Divide. Then multiply.

$$\begin{array}{r} 221 \\ 12\overline{)2,654} \\ -24\downarrow \\ \hline 25 \\ -24 \\ \hline 14 \\ 12 \end{array}$$

Step 7
Subtract and compare.

$$\begin{array}{r} 221 \text{ R2}\\ 12\overline{)2,654} \\ -24 \\ \hline 25 \\ -24 \\ \hline 14 \\ -12 \\ \hline 2 \end{array}$$

Step 8
Check your answer.

$$\begin{array}{r} 221 \quad \text{quotient}\\ \times\quad 12 \quad \text{divisor}\\ \hline 442 \\ +2210 \\ \hline 2652 \\ +\quad\ 2 \quad \text{remainder}\\ \hline 2,654 \quad \text{dividend} \end{array}$$

Practice and Check

Tip: Watch for remainders.

Find each quotient and check.

Check

Check

Check

$12\overline{)2{,}6\ 5\ 4}$ R

×

+

+ R

$12\overline{)1{,}8\ 4\ 8}$ R

×

+

+ R

$10\overline{)3{,}8\ 7\ 2}$ R

×

+

+ R

$12\overline{)2{,}5\ 0\ 0}$ R

×

+

+ R

$11\overline{)2{,}7\ 9\ 5}$ R

×

+

+ R

$10\overline{)1{,}0\ 9\ 5}$ R

×

+

+ R

Review and Check

Find each quotient and check.

Check ↓

$$12 \overline{)2,656} \,^{R}$$

×
+
+

R

R

Check ↓

$$12 \overline{)4,972} \,^{R}$$

×
+
+

R

R

Check ↓

$$12 \overline{)3,755} \,^{R}$$

×
+
+

R

R

$$11 \overline{)4,882} \,^{R}$$

×
+
+

R

R

$$10 \overline{)2,573} \,^{R}$$

×
+
+

R

R

$$11 \overline{)7,778} \,^{R}$$

×
+
+

R

R

When you get all of the answers right, put a sticker on ★26 on your poster.

Overall Review and Check

Find each quotient and check.

$3\overline{)385}$ R

×
+
+

R

$10\overline{)2,454}$ R

×
+
+

R

$7\overline{)25}$ R

×
+
+

R

$12\overline{)5,477}$ R

×
+
+

R

$5\overline{)689}$ R

×
+
+

R

$7\overline{)98}$ R

×
+
+

R

Keep going! There's more!

Overall Review and Check

Find each quotient and check.

Check
↓

$7\overline{)8,123}$ ^R

×
+
+ R

Check
↓

$6\overline{)6,662}$ ^R

×
+
+ R

Check
↓

$12\overline{)7,272}$ ^R

×
+
+ R

$11\overline{)2,938}$ ^R

×
+
+ R

$9\overline{)6,105}$ ^R

×
+
+ R

$4\overline{)4,510}$ ^R

×
+
+ R

Keep going! There's more!

Overall Review and Check

Find each quotient and check.

Check ↓

$$5{\overline{\smash{)}9{,}084}}^{\text{R}}$$

×	
+	
+	R

Check ↓

$$9{\overline{\smash{)}603}}^{\text{R}}$$

×	
+	
+	R

Check ↓

$$12{\overline{\smash{)}2{,}662}}^{\text{R}}$$

×	
+	
+	R

$$8{\overline{\smash{)}409}}^{\text{R}}$$

×	
+	
+	R

$$8{\overline{\smash{)}7{,}158}}^{\text{R}}$$

×	
+	
+	R

$$7{\overline{\smash{)}331}}^{\text{R}}$$

×	
+	
+	R

When you get all of the answers right, put a sticker on ★27 on your poster.

Tip: These problems are more difficult. Make sure your child has mastered the previous pages before working on these exercises.

Advanced Problems

Find each quotient and check.

Check

$15\overline{)7,141}$ R ____

×
+
+	R

Check

$20\overline{)415}$ R ____

×
+
+	R

Check

$31\overline{)9,993}$ R ____

×
+
+	R

$44\overline{)4,518}$ R ____

×
+
+	R

$63\overline{)3,309}$ R ____

×
+
+	R

$91\overline{)1,004}$ R ____

×
+
+	R

Keep going! There's more!

Overall Review and Check

Tip: If your child is having trouble, review the problems on pages 86–89.

Advanced Problems

Find each quotient and check.

Check

$27\overline{)1{,}215}$ ᴿ

×	
+	
+	ᴿ

Check

$36\overline{)1{,}066}$ ᴿ

×	
+	
+	ᴿ

Check

$42\overline{)1{,}510}$ ᴿ

×	
+	
+	ᴿ

$88\overline{)9{,}020}$ ᴿ

×	
+	
+	ᴿ

$13\overline{)3{,}219}$ ᴿ

×	
+	
+	ᴿ

$23\overline{)9{,}900}$ ᴿ

×	
+	
+	ᴿ

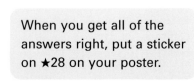

When you get all of the answers right, put a sticker on ★28 on your poster.

91

Overall Review and Check

Advanced Problems

Find each quotient and check.

Check

30)1,506
R

× |
--- |
+ |
+ | R
 |

Check

22)2,946
R

× |
--- |
+ |
+ | R
 |

Check

43)5,863
R

× |
--- |
+ |
+ | R
 |

18)3,674
R

× |
--- |
+ |
+ | R
 |

7)2,122
R

× |
--- |
+ |
+ | R
 |

14)2,809
R

× |
--- |
+ |
+ | R
 |

Keep going! There's more!

92

Overall Review and Check

Advanced Problems

Find each quotient and check.

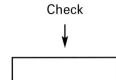

Check

Check

Check

$$39\overline{)1{,}083}^{\text{R}}$$

× |
+ |
+ | R
|

$$12\overline{)6{,}544}^{\text{R}}$$

× |
+ |
+ | R
|

$$4\overline{)3{,}655}^{\text{R}}$$

× |
+ |
+ | R
|

$$13\overline{)6{,}338}^{\text{R}}$$

× |
+ |
+ | R
|

$$10\overline{)9{,}494}^{\text{R}}$$

× |
+ |
+ | R
|

$$27\overline{)4{,}132}^{\text{R}}$$

× |
+ |
+ | R
|

When you get all of the answers right, put a sticker on ★29 on your poster.

I did it!

✦ Congratulations ✦
on finishing Workbook 4, Division!

Congratulations! You've completed the **Hooked on Math** • **Master the Facts** program.
Be sure to send in the postcard for your child's certificate of completion.

The answer to the puzzle on page 83: This number can be divided by every number from 1 to 16 with no remainders! Even better, it has every number in it—from 1 to 9!